Go and Make Disciples

A National Plan and Strategy for Catholic Evangelization in the United States

United States Catholic Conference

Washington, D.C.

In March 1990, the Committee on Evangelization of the National Conference of Catholic Bishops presented plans to develop a national plan and strategy for evangelization to the NCCB Administrative Committee. After conducting a broad consultation with dioceses, state Catholic conferences, religious communities, and national organizations, the Committee on Evangelization submitted a final draft to the plenary assembly of the National Conference of Catholic Bishops. *Go and Make Disciples: A National Plan and Strategy for Catholic Evangelization in the United States* was approved on November 18, 1992, and is hereby authorized for publication by the undersigned.

Monsignor Robert N. Lynch
General Secretary
NCCB/USCC

All photographs used within this text are by Michael Hoyt/Catholic Standard; Washington, D.C.

ISBN 1-55586-556-9

Sixth Printing, January 1996

Contents

Dedication

Fr. Alvin Illig, CSP, devoted his life to the task that Pope Paul VI called "the essential mission of the Church." Touched by the Holy Spirit, he labored to spread the Gospel of Jesus Christ and the truth of the Catholic faith before the duty to evangelize was widely accepted. He led the way for the rest of us.

Fr. Illig is best known as founding director of the Paulist National Catholic Evangelization Association. However, he also served as first executive director of the NCCB Committee on Evangelization from 1977 to 1982, doing everything in his power to ensure that the whole Church in the United States lived and preached the Good News.

It was Fr. Illig's generous support that enabled the committee to write this National Plan and Strategy. In recognition of his service to the Church and to the cause of Catholic evangelization, we hereby dedicate it to him. May it serve as a fitting memorial to one ever faithful to the Lord.

"Go, therefore, and make disciples of all nations, baptizing them in the name of the Father, and of the Son, and of the holy Spirit, teaching them to observe all that I have commanded you. And behold, I am with you always, until the end of the age" (Mt 28:19-20).

"I have come to set the earth on fire, and how I wish it were already blazing" (Lk 12:49).

Jesus set the world on fire, and that blaze goes on even today. Here is Bartimaeus, blind and begging on the roadside; he hears of Jesus and, no matter what, will not stop shouting until Jesus stops to heal him. Once healed, he follows Jesus.[1] Or the unnamed centurion, not even a Jew, whose servant is dying. "I am not worthy," he says. Jesus' command saves the servant's life. And the depth of the centurion's faith astonishes even Jesus.[2] The woman of Samaria goes to get water; after she meets Jesus and feels his kindness, she opens her soul and her pain to him. Not only does she believe—she must tell others as well![3] Or Jesus' friends, the family of Mary, Martha, and Lazarus: the sisters would often welcome Jesus into their house; and when Lazarus died, Jesus wept, but then put his tears aside, and raised him. "This caused many to believe."[4] Each of these people, touched by Christ Jesus, responded to him and so became part of the story of salvation.

We have heard these, and so many other gospel stories of Jesus Sunday after Sunday at church, in our own reading and sharing of Scriptures, in the words mothers and fathers tell their children, in the private meditation of our prayer, in the celebration of the sacraments. We have become, through the power and truth of these stories, and through the free gift of grace, disciples of Jesus.

We have heard them, and they will not let us rest. They burn, and they still set us ablaze!

Part I
A Vision of Catholic Evangelization

Introduction

We present to you, our Catholic sisters and brothers, this plan and strategy of evangelization because the fire of Jesus burns even today. We, your brothers and your bishops, profess our faith in Christ Jesus, in the revelation that he is and the kingdom that he proclaimed, and in the Church he founded. We proclaim that, through our faith, the stories of Christ continue and that our lives, as believers, are part of the story of salvation.

We say it about ourselves as bishops: God has touched our lives in Jesus, bestowed his Spirit, given us salvation and hope, and called us to live in witness to his love.

We know this is true of you as well: you have received the Spirit of Christ Jesus, which brings salvation and hope; your lives are a witness of faith. Whether you were baptized as a child or joined the Church as an adult, you have a story of faith. Whether you sincerely live your faith in quiet or have a great public ministry, you have a story of faith. Whether you have a grade-school knowledge of the catechism or have a theological degree, you have a story of faith.

We all have—and are—stories of faith, for through the Spirit, the Gospel of Jesus Christ takes hold of us in the proclamation of his word, and Jesus touches us in the celebration of his sacraments. When this genuinely happens, we are all set ablaze by his love.

We can understand evangelization in light of these stories of faith: namely, how we have been changed by the power of Christ's word and sacraments and how we have an essential role in sharing that faith through our daily lives as believers. Looked at this way, evangelization is what we are all about! Being involved in the story of salvation is what faith is all about! Evangelization is the essential mission of the Church.[5]

As we begin this plan and strategy, we turn in prayer to the Holy Spirit, that we may receive the guidance we need to set the hearts of Catholics in the United States on fire with a desire to bring the Gospel of Jesus, in its fullness, to all the people of our land.

What Is Evangelization?

The simplest way to say what evangelization means is to follow Pope Paul VI, whose message *On Evangelization in the Modern World* has inspired so much recent thought and activity. We can rephrase his words by saying that evangelizing means bringing the Good News of Jesus into every human situation and seeking to convert individuals and society by the divine power of the Gospel itself.[6] Its essence is the proclamation of salvation in Jesus Christ and the response of a person in faith, both being the work of the Spirit of God.

Evangelization must always be directly connected to the Lord Jesus Christ. "There is no true evangelization if the name, the teaching, the promises, the Kingdom and the mystery of Jesus of Nazareth, the Son of God are not proclaimed."[7]

Conversion

Conversion is the change of our lives that comes about through the power of the Holy Spirit. All who accept the Gospel undergo change as we continually put on the mind of Christ by rejecting sin and becoming more faithful disciples in his Church. Unless we undergo conversion, we have not truly accepted the Gospel.

We know that people experience conversion in many ways. Some experience a sudden, shattering insight that brings rapid transformation. Some experience a gradual growth over many years. Others undergo conversion as they take part in the Rite of Christian Initiation of Adults—the normal way adults become members of the Church today. Many experience conversion through the ordinary relationships of family and friends. Others have experienced it through the

formation received from Catholic schools and religious education programs. Still others have experienced ongoing conversion in renewals, ecumenical encounters, retreats, parish missions, or through some of the great spiritual movements that have blessed church life today.

This is crucial: we must be converted—and we must continue to be converted! We must let the Holy Spirit change our lives! We must respond to Jesus Christ. And we must be open to the transforming power of the Holy Spirit who will continue to convert us as we follow Christ. If our faith is alive, it will be aroused again and again as we mature as disciples.

We can only share what we have received; we can hold on to our faith only if it continues to grow. "But if salt loses its taste," Jesus asked, "with what can it be seasoned?"[8]

Individuals and Society

The continuing story of salvation in Christ involves each of us one by one as well as society itself. How else could it be? Conversion speaks of the change of heart that, as members of the Church, each one must undergo. The Gospel speaks across time and space to each human being, each mind, each heart. It asks us what we think about our lives, how we hope, whom we love, and what we live for. If faith is not transforming each heart and life, it is dead.

But faith is not something that only happens to each of us individually or privately, within ourselves. The Gospel also speaks to society itself, with its values, goals, and systems. The Gospel must overflow from each heart until the presence of God transforms all human existence. Sometimes this means that, as believers, we must confront the world as did the prophets of old, pointing out the claims of God to societies that are blind to God. More often, however, this means that we must let our faith shine on the world around us, radiating the love of Jesus by the everyday way we speak, think, and act.

The fruit of evangelization is changed lives and a changed world—holiness and justice, spirituality and peace. The validity of our having accepted the Gospel does not only come from what we feel or what we know; it comes also from the way we serve others, especially the poorest, the most marginal, the most hurting, the most defenseless, the least loved. An evangelization that stays inside ourselves is not an evangelization into the Good News of Jesus Christ.

The Force of the Gospel Itself

Evangelization happens when the word of Jesus speaks to people's hearts and minds. Needing no trickery or manipulation, evangelization can happen only when people accept the Gospel freely, as the "good news" it is meant to be, because of the power of the gospel message and the accompanying grace of God.

Our message of faith proclaims an eternally faithful God, creating all in love and sustaining all with gracious care. We proclaim that God, whose love is unconditional, offers us divine life even in the face of our sin, failures, and inadequacies. We believe in a God who became one of us in Jesus, God's Son, whose death and resurrection bring us salvation. We believe that the risen Christ sends his own Spirit upon us when we respond to him in faith and repentance, making us his people, the Church, and giving us the power of new life and guiding us to our eternal destiny.

This gospel message gives us a different vision of what life is about. We see a pattern of love, hope, and meaning because the intimate relationship with God in which we were created, lost through sin, has been restored by Jesus, whose death has destroyed our death and whose resurrection gives us the promise of eternal life.[9] We do not see a world of blind forces ruled by chance, but a universe created to share God's life; we know that following Jesus means we begin to share God's life here and now. We do not view life's purpose as the gathering of power or riches, but as the gracious invitation to live for God and others in love. We do not calculate what we think is possible, but know the Spirit of God always makes new things possible, even the renewal of humanity. We do not merely look for many years of contented life, but for an unending life of happiness with God. In our faith, we discover God's eternal plan, from creation's first moment to creation's fulfillment in heaven, giving meaning to our human lives.

This vision we share is the power of the Good News. As it compels us, we believe it can compel, by its beauty and truth, all who sincerely seek God. How different our world would be if everyone could accept the Good News of Jesus and share the vision of faith!

Other Implications

Evangelization, then, has both an inward and an outward direction. *Inwardly,* it calls for our continued receiving of the Gospel of Jesus Christ, our ongoing conversion both individually and as Church. It nurtures us, makes us grow, and renews us in holiness as God's people. *Outwardly,* evangelization addresses those who have not heard the Gospel or, having heard it, have stopped practicing their faith, and those who seek the fullness of faith. It calls us to work for full communion among all who confess Jesus, but do not yet realize the unity for which Christ prayed. Pope John Paul II, in his encyclical on missionary activity, summed up the three objectives of mission: to proclaim the Gospel to all people; to help bring about the reconversion of those who have received the Gospel but live it only nominally; and to deepen the Gospel in the lives of believers.[10]

We know that the word *evangelization* sometimes raises uncomfortable images for Catholics —especially in the culture of the United States, where evangelism has sometimes meant only an individual response to enthusiastic preaching or a style of mass religion or contrived ways to recruit new members or, at its worst, a way to play on people's needs. Still, we use the word *evangelization* because its root meaning is *Gospel* (good news) and because it calls us, even if uncomfortably, to live the faith of our baptism more openly and share it more freely.

We evangelize so that the salvation of Christ Jesus, which transforms our human lives even now, will bring as many as possible to the promised life of unending happiness in heaven.

We want to make it clear that evangelization means something special for us as Catholics. We can see what it means by looking at what happens to evangelized people. Not only are they related to Jesus by accepting his Gospel and receiving his Spirit; even more, their lives are changed by becoming disciples, that is, participants in the Church, celebrating God's love in worship and serving others as Jesus did.[11]

Some might think of evangelization solely in terms of Jesus and our relationship with him. Yet our relationship with Jesus is found in our relationship with the community of Jesus—the Church. The way to Christ is through the community in which he lives. Did not Jesus say, "I am with you always"[12] and "Whatever you did for one of these least" brothers and sisters of mine, "you did for me"?[13] Did not the Jesus who met Paul on the road to Damascus say that he lived in his persecuted followers, the Church?[14] Jesus is present in and among his disciples, the People of God.

Evangelization, then, has different implications depending on our relationship to Jesus and his Church. For those of us who practice and live our Catholic faith, it is a call to ongoing growth and renewed conversion. For those who have accepted it only in name, it is a call to reevangelization. For those who have stopped practicing their faith, it is a call to reconciliation. For children, it is a call to be formed into disciples through the family's faith life and religious education. For other Christians, it is an invitation to know the fullness of our message. For those who have no faith, it is a call to conversion to know Christ Jesus and thus experience a change to new life with Christ and his Church.

Why We Evangelize

We must evangelize because the Lord Jesus commanded us to. He gave the Church the unending task of evangelizing as a restless power, to stir and to stimulate all its actions until all nations have heard his Good News and until every person has become his disciple.[15]

The Lord commanded us to evangelize because salvation is offered to every person in him. More than a holy figure or a prophet, Jesus is God's Word,[16] God's "very imprint,"[17] the power and wisdom of God.[18] He is our savior. Becoming like us and accepting our human nature,[19] he addresses in himself, in his death and resurrection, the brokenness of our lives. He suffers through our sin; he feels our pain; he knows the thirst of our death; he accepts the limits of our human life so that he might bring us beyond those limits. "[H]e humbled himself, becoming obedient to death, even death on a cross. Because of this, God greatly exalted him! . . ."[20] Taking on our death as savior, Jesus was raised to life. In Christ, all can come to know that the sin, the coldness, the indifference, the despair, and the doubt of our lives are overcome by God's taking on our human nature and leading us to new life. In him, and him alone, is the promise of resurrection and new life.

We evangelize because people must be brought to the salvation Jesus the Lord offers in and through the Church. While we acknowledge that the grace of God is mysteriously present in all lives, people all too often resist this grace. They refuse change and repentance. We evangelize so that the salvation of Christ Jesus, which transforms our human lives even now, will bring as many as possible to the promised life of unending happiness in heaven.

Jesus commanded us to evangelize, too, in order to bring enlightenment and lift people from error. The Lord Jesus, "the way and the truth and the life,"[21] came to us as a teacher, opening for us the wisdom that not only leads to life eternal but also leads to a human fulfillment that reflects the dignity and mystery of our nature. Unless people know the grandeur for which they are made, they cannot reach fulfillment and their lives will be incomplete. Nor will they know that they are called into interpersonal union with God and with each other. The intimate union that Jesus revealed in his life, being one with the Father[22] and rejoicing in the Holy Spirit,[23] can envelop our lives. This is the union in which Jesus wishes all to share,[24] a union whose realization brings great peace to people, families, societies, and the world. Evangelization opens us to Christ's wisdom and personal union with God and others.

The Lord gave us a message that is unique. All faiths are not merely different versions of the same thing. To know Christ Jesus and belong to his Church is not the same as believing anything and belonging to any community. Pope John Paul II has pointed out, "While acknowledging that God loves all people and grants them the possibility of being saved (cf. 1 Tm 2:4), the Church believes that God has established Christ as the one mediator and that she herself has been established as the universal sacrament of salvation."[25] The unique claim of our message does not negate the sincerity and faith of others; likewise, the sincerity and faith of others do not take away from the clarity and truth of our message. As Pope John Paul II reminds us, "It is necessary to keep these two truths together, namely, the real possibility of salvation in Christ for all humankind and the necessity of the Church for salvation. Both these truths help us to understand the one mystery of salvation."[26]

Finally, the Lord gave us yet another reason to evangelize: our love for every person, whatever his or her situation, language, physical, mental, or social condition. Because we have experienced the love of Christ, we want to share it. The gifts God has given to us are not gifts for ourselves. Like the large catch of fish[27] or the overflowing measure of flour,[28] our faith makes our hearts abound with a love-filled desire to bring all people to Jesus' Gospel and to the table of the Eucharist. As Jesus wanted to gather all Jerusalem, "like a hen gathers her young,"[29] so also do we want to gather all people into God's kingdom, proclaiming the Gospel "even to the ends of the earth."[30]

How Evangelization Happens

The Holy Spirit is the fire of Jesus. The Spirit, the first gift of the risen Christ to his people,[31] gives us both the ability to receive the Gospel of Jesus and, in response, the power to proclaim it. Without the Holy Spirit, evangelization simply cannot occur.[32] The Spirit brings about evangelization in the life of the Church and in the Church's sharing the Gospel with others.

In the Life of the Church

We cannot really talk about the "ordinary" life of the Church because all of it is the graced gift of the Holy Spirit. Yet there are familiar ways by which evangelization happens: by the way we live God's love in our daily life; by the love, example, and support people give each other; and by the ways parents pass faith on to their children; in our life as Church, through the proclamation of the word and the wholehearted celebration of the saving deeds of Jesus; in renewal efforts of local and national scope; in the care we show to those most in need; in the ways we go about our work, share with our neighbors, and treat the stranger. In daily life, family members evangelize each other, men and women their future spouses, and workers their fellow employees by the simple lives of faith they lead. Through the ordinary patterns of our Catholic life, the Holy Spirit brings about conversion and a new life in Christ.

Here, there are two elements at work: *witness,* which is the simple living of the faith; and *sharing,* which is spreading the Good News of Jesus in an explicit way.

Certainly, our families, parishes, associations, schools, hospitals, charitable works, and institutions give powerful witness to the faith. But do they share it? Does their living faith lead to the conversion of minds and hearts to Jesus Christ? Does the fire of the Holy Spirit blaze in them? This plan and strategy wants to make Catholics in the United States, individually and as a Church, better sharers of God's Good News.

In Sharing the Gospel with Others

The Holy Spirit also evangelizes through our attempts to reach those who have given up the practice of their Catholic faith for one reason or another and those who have no family of faith. Many in our Catholic community know family members, friends, and neighbors who do not have or practice faith.

Millions of Catholics no longer practice their faith. Although may of them may say they are Catholic, they no longer worship with the community and thereby deprive themselves of the gifts of Word and sacrament. Some were never formed in the faith after their childhood. Some have drifted away because of one or another issue. Some feel alienated from the Church because of the way they perceive the Church or its teaching. Some have left because they were mistreated by church representatives.

As a community of faith, we want to welcome these people to become alive in the Good News of Jesus, to make their lives more fully a part of the ongoing story of salvation and to let Christ touch, heal, and reconcile them through the Holy Spirit. We want to let our inactive brothers and sisters know that they always have a place in the Church and that we are hurt by their absence—as they are. We want to show our regret for any misunderstandings or mistreatment. And we want to help them see that, however they feel about the Church, we want to talk with them, share with them, and accept them as brothers and sisters. Every Catholic can be a minister of welcome, reconciliation, and understanding to those who have stopped practicing the faith.

The Spirit, the first gift of the risen Christ to his people, gives us both the ability to receive the Gospel of Jesus and, in response, the power to proclaim it.

Our plan also asks Catholics to reach out to those who do not belong to a faith community and to invite them to consider the power of the Gospel of Jesus, which the riches of the Catholic Church can bring into their lives. Perhaps this may seem the most difficult of all the tasks evangelization asks of us. Yet if we have once seen the joy of those received into the Church at Easter, if we have ever experienced the growth of those going through the Rite of Christian Initiation of Adults, if we have ever seen someone thrilled with the Gospel for the first time in his or her life, we know that this is, in truth, one of the sweetest gifts of the Spirit.

The Holy Spirit, through the ecumenical movement, is calling churches and ecclesial communities into ever deeper communion through dialogue and cooperation. We look forward with great eagerness to the day when all are members of one family. While recognizing that the life of other Christian communions can truly bring about a life of grace, we nevertheless cannot ignore all that still divides us. Our love for all who confess Christ and our desire for unity compel us to share the fullness of revealed truth God has entrusted to the Catholic Church and to learn from them expressions of the truths of faith that other churches and ecclesial communities share with the Catholic Church.

Those who have not received the Gospel

deserve honor and respect for following God as their consciences direct them. They are related to the People of God in a variety of ways. First are the Jews, the Chosen People, to whom the covenants and promises were made and who, in view of the divine choice, are a people most dear to God.

People of other non-Christian religions also have the right to hear the Gospel, as missionaries have brought it over the centuries. God's plan of salvation also includes the Muslims who profess the faith of Abraham and, together with us, adore the one, merciful God. Then there are those who through no fault of their own do not know the Gospel of Christ or his Church but nevertheless seek God with sincere heart and seek to do God's will as they know it. Interreligious dialogue presents an opportunity to learn about other religious traditions and to explain our own. Such dialogue, however, must never be a camouflage for proselytizing. Rather, it should be approached with utmost respect and sensitivity. Catholics earnestly share their faith in Jesus Christ, which gives meaning to their lives, praying for that good day, known to God alone, when all peoples will address the Lord in a single voice and serve God with one accord.[33]

Our Goals

We, your brothers and your bishops in the faith, propose three goals as part of this plan and strategy for Catholic evangelization in the United States. In addition, we pledge ourselves to work for the accomplishment of these goals, which spring from our understanding of evangelization and how it happens. None of these goals is presented by itself; taken together, they challenge us to the full scope of Catholic evangelization.

> *Goal I: To bring about in all Catholics such an enthusiasm for their faith that, in living their faith in Jesus, they freely share it with others.*

Clearly, unless we continue to be evangelized ourselves, with renewed enthusiasm for our faith and our Church, we cannot evangelize others. Priority must be given to continued and renewed formation in the faith as the basis of our deepening personal relationship with Jesus.

We are aware that many Catholics tend to keep their faith to themselves or to manifest it only around other Catholics. Perhaps our heritage as immigrants and our acknowledgment of religious pluralism make us shy in showing forth our faith. Certainly, there has also been a decline in the public practice of our faith in recent decades. For many, the fire of faith burns cooler than it should.

Yet we have no reason to be shy about the heritage of our Catholic faith. We have God's own Word, formed through God's revelation to the Jewish people and the disciples' testimony of God's deeds in Jesus, in the Sacred Scriptures. This Word is the light by which we live and see. We have the sacraments, especially the Eucharist, Jesus bequeathed to his disciples, means of holiness and growth, healing and salvation. These sacraments join us with God at life's most touching points and bring us into unity with each other. This heritage of Word and sacrament has brought about, in every generation of our twenty centuries of Catholic life, a path of holiness, a profoundly moral way of life, a variety of spiritual journeys, and countless saints. It brings Christ's faithful followers to eternal life.

This heritage, our Church, is apostolic, coming as it does from the testimony of the apostles; our unbroken unity with the bishop of Rome reveals our continuity with the faith of Peter and Paul. It is catholic, for our heritage is given not only for us but for all, for the world, as the hope of all humanity one day united in love. It is holy, because its source is Christ who is holy and insists that every believer also be a disciple. And our heritage is one, binding us in every continent into one community because we are bound in nothing less than the reality of Jesus through his Spirit.

Our joy in this heritage calls us to offer it as a legacy, a treasure God would bestow on everyone who, touched by the Spirit, begins to respond to God's call. The tools that have been developed over time and the *Catechism of the Catholic Church* will help us pass on this legacy to others.

This first goal calls us to an enthusiasm for all that God has given us in our Catholic faith. It also fosters ongoing conversion within the Catholic Church which, as an institution and a community of people, it continually needs.

Goal II: To invite all people in the United States, whatever their social or cultural background, to hear the message of salvation in Jesus Christ so they may come to join us in the fullness of the Catholic faith.

Catholics should continually share the Gospel with those who have no church community, with those who have given up active participation in the Catholic Church, as well as welcoming those seeking full communion with the Catholic Church. People can know they are invited to experience Jesus Christ in our Church only if they are really and effectively asked and adequate provisions are made for their full participation. We want our Catholic brothers and sisters to effectively ask and to really invite.

At the same time, we Catholics cannot proselytize—that is, manipulate or pressure anyone to join our Church. Such tactics contradict the Good News we announce and undermine the spirit of invitation that should characterize all true evangelization.

Goal III: To foster gospel values in our society, promoting the dignity of the human person, the importance of the family, and the common good of our society, so that our nation may continue to be transformed by the saving power of Jesus Christ.

When the story of Jesus is truly our story, when we have caught his fire, when his Good News shapes our lives individually, as families and households, and as a Church, his influence will be felt far beyond our Church. Pope Paul VI taught us that evangelization transforms culture, that the Gospel affects and at times upsets the "criteria of judgment, determining values,

points of interest, lines of thought, sources of inspiration and models of life" that make up our cultural world.[34]

Not only must each of us live the Gospel personally in the Church, but our faith must touch the values of the United States, affirming what is good, courageously challenging what is not. Catholics applaud our nation's instinctual religiousness, its prizing of freedom and religious liberty, its openness to new immigrants and its inspiring idealism. If our society were less open, indeed, we might not be free to evangelize in the first place. On the other hand, our country can be faulted for its materialism, sexism, racism, consumerism, its individualism run wild, its ethic of selfishness, its ignoring of the poor and weak, its disregard of human life, and its endless chase of empty fads and immediate pleasures.

Seeing both the ideals and the faults of our nation, we Catholics need to recognize how much our Catholic faith, for all it has received from American culture, still has to bring to life in our country. On the level of truth, we have a profound and consistent moral teaching based upon the dignity and destiny of every person created by God. On the practical level, we have the witness of American Catholics serving those most in need, educationally, socially, materially, and spiritually.

This goal calls for results not only in the way we evaluate things but also in the way we carry Good News through the practical works of justice, charity, and peace which alone can fully authenticate our message. With Pope John Paul II, we affirm that "[T]o teach and spread her social doctrine pertains to the Church's evangelizing mission and is an essential part of the Christian message, since this doctrine points out the direct consequences of that message in the life of society and situates daily work and struggles for justice in the context of bearing witness to Christ the savior."[35]

Why We Are Issuing the Plan Now

Since the turn of this century, the Holy Spirit has inspired great events to further evangelization in the Church. A new appreciation of the Scriptures and the mystery of our sharing in the Body of Christ, the Church, flowered into the Second Vatican Council which was called so that the face of Jesus might radiate more fully upon all.[36] This Council brought a renewed sense of faith and worship, a commitment to ecumenical unity, an affirmation of the call to holiness that each one has, and a new emphasis on evangelization. This Council has changed the way we live our Catholic faith. Following the Council in 1974, bishops from all over the world met in Rome to reflect on evangelization; their reflections were expressed by Pope Paul VI in his apostolic exhortation, *On Evangelization in the Modern World*. Pope John Paul II has developed further the awareness of evangelization. Recognizing the need from his global travels, he called for a "new evangelization" in 1983 and called for lay people to become involved in evangelization.[37] In 1991, the pope published his eighth encyclical, *Redemptoris Missio, On the Permanent Validity of the Church's Missionary Mandate*. The Holy Father's powerful words call us to a renewed commitment to mission and evangelization as we come to the final decade of this millennium: "I sense that the moment has come to commit all of the Church's energies to a new evangelization. . . ."[38]

We bishops have dealt with the importance of evangelization in our statements. A wide consultation among Hispanic Catholics resulted in the publication of the *National Pastoral Plan for Hispanic Ministry*[39] to address issues relevant to the many Hispanic peoples entering and enriching our nation. Likewise, our African American brothers and sisters have worked on a pastoral plan entitled *Here I Am, Send Me: A Conference Response to the Evangelization of African Americans and "The National Black Catholic Pastoral Plan,"*[40] that speaks from their cultural uniqueness and is a gift to all of us. In our own recent pastoral statement, *Heritage and Hope: Evangelization in the United States,*[41] we explored the meaning of the five hundredth anniversary (1492-1992) of Christopher Columbus' voyage to the New World. While all Christians deeply regret the disease, death, exploitation, and cultural devastation European settlement brought, we rejoice that missionaries carried the light of Christ and were the first to raise their voices against oppression. That first evangelization planted the faith that we now seek to nurture.

All this movement and all these documents call us to reexamine our hearts and recommit our wills to the pursuit of evangelization; they motivate us to issue this plan to make evangelization a natural and normal part of Catholic life and to give evangelizers the tools and support they need to carry out this ministry today.

Led in the Spirit

*O*ne day Jesus left Galilee and went to the River Jordan where he saw his kinsman, John the Baptist, calling people to repentance and renewal. He stepped forth from the crowd and approached John for baptism. John hesitated, recognizing the uniqueness of Jesus. When Jesus insisted, John plunged him into the water. At that point, people heard a voice from the clouds; John saw the Spirit come upon Jesus who was being revealed at this moment by God as the "Chosen One."[42]

The Spirit drove Jesus out into the desert[43] and, after a while, into a ministry that began with Jesus addressing simple fishermen and small groups of people in his homeland. The Spirit led Jesus on a journey through Palestine to Jerusalem where his message came to challenge the whole world.

Jesus was led by the Spirit of God to a life of preaching and service, to the giving of himself in sacrifice. Jesus Christ sends that same Spirit upon everyone who is baptized in his name. For we have all gone down into the water of Christ and have all been anointed to bring Good News and be true disciples.[44] We have all received his Spirit. This is not a Spirit of timidity or fear, but a bold Spirit of life, truth, joy, and grace.

We, bishops and Catholic people, are all led by this same Spirit who would stir up the faithful in our land to bring about a new and powerful evangelization. With Jesus, we undertake this journey, knowing that he is with us and his Spirit can never fail.

Jesus came to set this fire upon the earth, until all is ablaze in the love of God. We pray this fire will come upon us as disciples as we, led by the Spirit, carry out Christ's great commission to go and make disciples of all the nations.

Part II
Goals and Strategies

*N*ot long after Jesus was raised from the dead, a small group huddled together in a secluded room. Suddenly, the building shook, a great wind encircled them, and flames of fire, like tongues, appeared around the group.[45]

We see, in the midst of this small group, two people whose lives still guide us in the work of evangelization. We see a woman, Mary, now middle-aged, who, over thirty years before, was overshadowed by the Holy Spirit and became the mother of Jesus.[46] God used the faith of this Jewish woman, her cooperation with God's way, to bring Jesus into the world. So Mary, long devoutly loved by Christians as the Mother of Jesus and Mother of God, also is a model of true discipleship and evangelization. With Mary's example and prayer, we grow as disciples, ever faithful to Jesus and ever wanting to reveal him.

We also see a former fisherman, now called Peter, whom Jesus chose to give as a leader to the disciples.[47] Though weak enough to deny his friend Jesus,[48] he is yet empowered to proclaim the faith of Jesus as Messiah.[49] He would proclaim that message until he died in testimony for the faith.[50] Jesus made Peter the "rock" of the Church and his faithfulness to the Lord, in spite of his weakness, strengthens us disciples today.

Two people, Mary and Peter, encircled by the other disciples, receive in the tongues of flame at Pentecost a confirmation of their discipleship, of their involvement in the story of Jesus, of their role in spreading God's Good News.[51]

This is the fire of the Holy Spirit from whom all evangelization springs. May the Spirit that came upon Mary and filled the apostles also come upon us as we present the apostolic parts of our plan.

How to Use This Plan and Strategy

Our hope, upon issuing this plan and strategy, is that it will lead Catholics to action. The goals, though broad, speak of the way we live our faith. The objectives, which follow each goal, expand those goals into several separate parts. The suggested strategies elaborate in more detail some of the ways of working at the objectives and goals.

We envision groups of Catholics reading this plan together, discussing its implications, and being stimulated by the range of suggested strategies. We see these groups seeking to do things, both within and beyond their own Catholic communities, in ways that make sense for their locale and situation. This document should generate discussion about action: the possibilities and activities present in every Catholic parish and institution.

Parish councils and parish evangelization teams should be able to use this plan and strategy to sharpen a parish's mission and develop concrete, suitable evangelizing activities. People who work in unchurched or marginalized areas will carry out this plan and strategy in less structured settings than those who work in large suburban parishes. Youth groups will read the document from their special situation in life and think about how to reach peers in convincing ways. On college campuses, students and campus ministers can form groups to see what the goals of this document mean on today's campuses. Catholics who share the same workplace may form a group that supports their own faith, strengthens them to invite people with whom they work, and also explores how their faith bears upon their occupation.

Individuals, too, should be led beyond insight and reflection into a range of actions that can be done in the home, the workplace, the neighborhood, and the civic setting. Each one's personal gifts and unique setting call for unique approaches in sharing faith.

Our presentation can only suggest the richness of this ministry. In fact, at the end of this plan we explicitly invite additional responses to the objectives we are setting forth. We look for innovative responses, far exceeding the suggested strategies we offer in this plan. The ministry of evangelization does not consist in following a recipe but in letting the Spirit open our hearts to God's word so that we can live and proclaim God's word to others. So, let the Spirit work!

The Context of the Goals

These goals are addressed to *all Catholics* in our country: to every diocese and every parish; to every Catholic person and to every family; to the ordained, religious women and men, and the laity; to the professional religious worker and ordinary parishioner; to large national organizations of Catholics and to every parish committee; to institutions like our Catholic colleges, high schools, and grade schools as well as to associations of the faithful. Although everyone will pursue these goals with different gifts, no one can claim exemption from them.

These goals are meaningless unless they are steeped in *prayer*. Without prayer, the Good News of Jesus Christ cannot be understood, spread, or accepted. These goals can be accomplished only by opening our hearts to God, who gives to his children everything they seek,[52] who responds when we knock, and who answers when we persevere in asking.[53] At Mass, in the Liturgy of the Hours, in prayer groups and individual prayer and devotions, we must ask unceasingly for the grace to evangelize. The moment we stop praying for the grace to spread the Good News of Jesus will be the moment when we lose the power to evangelize.

These goals also are issued in accord with the ministry of evangelization that belongs to the *whole Catholic Church*. This plan, the product of our reflection in the United States, adapts to our situation the missionary goals of Christ's Church throughout the world. They are offered in union with all Catholics everywhere, with their bishops, and the Holy Father, the Vicar of Christ, the bishop of Rome, the city of the apostles Peter and Paul. Unless evangelization is done in the context of this universal Catholic community, it is incomplete.[54] We urge this spirit upon our Catholic brothers and sisters.

These goals must bear upon our *everyday life*, in the family and the workplace, in our neighborhoods and associations, in the way we live. Catholics will be able to affect people in everyday life long before they are invited to a parish or to a formal religious event. All evangelization planning basically strives to make more possible the kind of everyday exchange between believers and unbelievers, which is the thrust of evangelization.

The *parish* is the most fitting location for carrying out these goals because the parish is where most Catholics experience the Church. It has, on the local level, the same commitments as the universal Church, with the celebration of God's word and Eucharist as its center of worship. Evangelization inevitably involves the parish community for, ultimately, we are inviting people to our Eucharist, to the table of the Lord. When an individual evangelizes, one to one, he or she should have the Good News and the eucharistic table as the ultimate focus.

These goals assume that an evangelizing spirit will touch every dimension of Catholic parish life. Welcome, acceptance, the invitation to conversion and renewal . . . must characterize the whole tenor of our parishes.

These goals assume that an evangelizing spirit will touch every dimension of Catholic parish life. Welcome, acceptance, the invitation to conversion and renewal, reconciliation and peace, beginning with our worship, must characterize the whole tenor of our parishes. Every element of the parish must respond to the evangelical imperative—priests and religious, lay persons, staff, ministers, organizations, social clubs, parochial schools, and parish religious education programs. Otherwise, evangelization will be something a few people in the parish see as their ministry—rather than the reason for the parish's existence and the objective of every ministry in the parish. The spirit of conversion, highlighted in the liturgy and particularly in the Rite of Christian Initiation of Adults, should radiate through the action of all Catholics so that the call to conversion is experienced and celebrated as part of our way of life.

Evangelization in the parish should be seen as a *collaborative* effort that springs from a partnership between the clergy and the laity. Priests have a special leadership role in carrying out this plan, but they should not feel isolated, overburdened, or frustrated in implementing it. Indeed, we even hope an increase in evangelizing will attract more people to the priesthood and religious life. The goals and strategies of our plan are not meant to be an added burden on already overworked pastoral staffs, as if evangelization were merely another program to be done. Rather, they should help parishes see the evangelizing potential of their current activities, even as they stretch parishes to develop new activities from a renewed spiritual energy.

These goals also call for a *consistency:* evangelization must affect the attitude of our Catholic life from top to bottom. We cannot call for renewal only on the parish level; we cannot proclaim mercy only for part of the year; we cannot welcome only some people. Everywhere Americans see Catholics and Catholic institutions they should sense the spirit of evangelization.

These goals, finally, will be carried out in the midst of a culture that will make them difficult to achieve. This difficulty will be, in part, a problem of communication because people may prefer stereotypes of the Catholic Church to a true picture of our faith. Another part of the difficulty will be social, because people will see the Catholic Church only as an organization of a certain economic class or educational level rather than as a richly varied and inviting community. Also, a superficial pluralism makes it hard for people to discuss faith seriously in our society. But most difficult of all will be the moral issues, which make the Good News hard to hear by people whose values are contrary to the Gospel and who must experience change in order to hear the message of life we proclaim.

Presentation of the Goals

Goal I: To bring about in all Catholics such an enthusiasm for their faith that, in living their faith in Jesus, they freely share it with others.

This goal calls Catholics to continue to hear the Good News at ever deeper levels. The call to holiness, given to every Catholic through baptism, consecrates each one to God and to the service of the kingdom.[55] This deepening of faith, in holiness, fosters a desire to involve others in that faith, until God will be "all in all" in a transformed world.[56]

The strategy of this goal is to so deepen the sense of Scripture and sacrament that Catholics will pray more fully, and, with a greater understanding of Christ's call, live as disciples at home, at work, and in today's many cultural settings. This goal also seeks a greater openness to physical, mental, and cultural diversity among Catholics.

This goal entails the following objectives:

❖ *To foster an experience of conversion and renewal in the heart of every believer, leading to a more active living of Catholic life.*

Possible strategies:

- retreats;
- parish renewals;
- RENEW;
- Cursillo;
- involvement in the Charismatic movement;
- youth encounter weekends;
- marriage encounter; and
- other programs of renewal and conversion.

❖ *To foster an experience of conversion and renewal in every parish.*

Possible strategies:

- expanded implementation of the Rite of Christian Initiation of Adults;
- wider invitation for Catholics to serve as sponsors; and
- parish involvement in ministries of reconciliation.

- *To foster an appreciation of God's word in the lives of all Catholics.*

  Possible strategies:
  - more frequent individual reading of the Bible among Catholics;
  - the further development of scriptural-study and scriptural-sharing programs; and
  - opportunities for more thorough scriptural studies on the part of all Catholics.

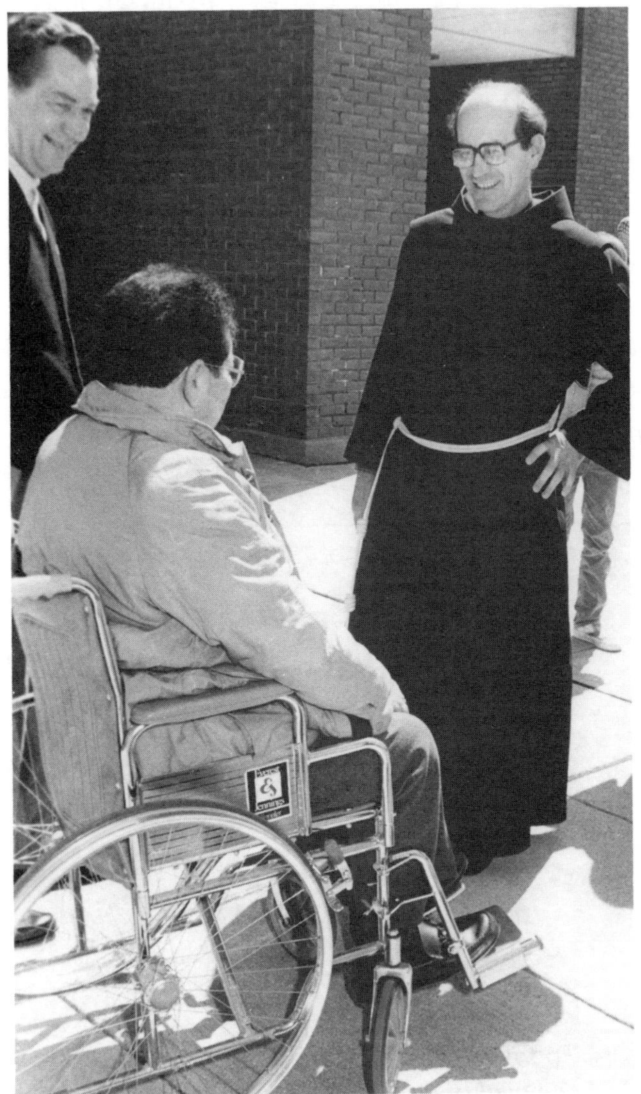

- *To make the evangelizing dimension of the Sunday Eucharist more explicit.*

  Possible strategies:
  - greeting and welcoming people;
  - creating a greater sense of prayer during Mass;
  - calling worshipers more clearly to conversion and renewal; fostering a sense of community among parish members; reaching out to visitors and newcomers at Sunday Mass;
  - making worship accessible to everyone; and
  - developing ways to incorporate new and mobile parishioners through ritual and public acknowledgment.

- *To foster an appreciation of the presence of Christ in the Eucharist and all the sacraments, the sacred signs of our Catholic life.*

  Possible strategies:
  - spirit-filled celebrations of the liturgy;
  - sacramental preparation programs;
  - encourage eucharistic devotions and adoration;
  - careful liturgical planning and ceremonial practice; and
  - renewal themes and activities centered on the sacraments.

- *To foster a greater appreciation of the power of God's word in our worship.*

  Possible strategies:
  - ongoing homiletic training for clergy and those called to preach;
  - prayerful preparation of the homily;
  - shared preparation of the Sunday homily;
  - enhanced preparation of lectors; and
  - special honor for the liturgical books that contain the Sacred Scriptures.

- *To foster an even deeper sense of prayer among our Catholic people.*

  Possible strategies:
  - a daily schedule of prayer for every Catholic;
  - wider utilization of the Liturgy of the Hours and other common prayer among Catholics;
  - prayer groups;
  - retreat experiences;
  - training in methods of meditation and contemplation; and
  - the publication of more accessible devotional reading.

- *To foster a renewed understanding of the faith among Catholics.*

  Possible strategies:
  - new methods of adult education, utilizing various modern media and relating to Catholics' involvement in parish worship and service;
  - formulation of catechetical material in clear, easy-to-grasp language;
  - revision of existing catechetical materials to facilitate evangelization and adapt the *Catechism of the Catholic Church* to the circumstances of the United States;
  - development of home and family-based catechetical techniques; and
  - involvement of directors of religious education in the evangelization planning of the parish and of evangelization teams in catechetical planning.

- *To foster a sense of discipleship among Catholic adults and children.*

  Possible strategies:
  - development of parochial and religious education curricula along the themes of discipleship with concentration on evangelization;
  - training for discipleship;
  - prayer events in parishes and larger Catholic organizations; and
  - more widespread involvement in ministry and service as part of the stewardship of gifts that God gives the Church.

- *To foster active and personal religious experience through participation in small-group and other communal experiences in which the Good News is shared, experienced, and applied to daily life.*

  Possible strategies:
  - prayer group development;
  - parish cultivation of smaller groupings for prayer, spiritual growth, and apostolic efforts;
  - prayer associations within parishes and large Catholic organizations; and
  - retreat experiences.

- *To foster a sense of the domestic church within households in which families, individuals, and groups reside.*

  Possible strategies:
  - cultivation of daily prayer and times of prayer in the home;
  - establishment of times of family sharing;
  - home-based rituals shaped by the liturgical year;
  - formation of groups of parents, families, and households to develop spirituality in the home; and
  - adaptation of new and meaningful faith practices within the family in view of the decline of family prayer.

- *To promote and develop a spirituality for the workplace.*

  Possible strategies:
  - to encourage reflection on the transforming presence of God in the workplace;
  - to acknowledge workers as agents of God's presence in the workplace; and
  - to encourage the formation of Catholic and other Christian groups and organizations that foster values in the workplace.

✤ *To foster greater appreciation of cultural and ethnic spirituality.*

Possible strategies:

- to celebrate the spiritual diversity of the different cultures that make up the Church in the United States;
- to acknowledge and respect various forms of personal piety;
- to celebrate cultural traditions; and
- to encourage a variety of musical and cultural expressions.

Goal II: To invite all people in the United States, whatever their social or cultural background, to hear the message of salvation in Jesus Christ so they may come to join us in the fullness of the Catholic faith.

This goal means that we are to invite effectively every person to come to know the Good News of Jesus proclaimed by the Catholic Church. This goal goes along with the first one for, as that goal is sought, Catholics will develop an inviting attitude as a general part of our everyday spirituality. This goal means not only that people are invited but also that an essential welcoming spirit is present in Catholic homes and in all our Catholic institutions: parishes, organizations, hospitals, schools, chanceries, and centers of neighborhood service. This goal also has ecumenical implications.

The strategy behind this goal is to create a more welcoming attitude toward others in our parishes so that people feel at home; next, to create an attitude of sharing faith and to develop greater skills to do this; then, to undertake activities to invite others to know the Catholic people better.

To attain this second goal, these objectives should be pursued:

✤ *To make every Catholic institution, especially our parishes, more welcoming.*

Possible strategies:

- review of the hospitality of our institutions;
- use of parochial schools and religious education programs for outreach and welcome for the whole family;
- greeting and welcoming workshops;
- retraining of ushers, receptionists, and other personnel; and
- study of the access and availability of our institutions to people (e.g., times, lighting, signs and posters, etc.), particularly with regard to welcoming the disabled (e.g., ramps into churches, adequate sound systems, signing for the hearing impaired, etc.).

✤ *To help every Catholic feel comfortable about sharing his or her faith and inviting people to discover Christ in our Catholic family of believers.*

Possible strategies:

- faith-sharing groups;
- training to discern religious experience and articulate it;
- development of a greater ability to listen and empathize; and
- encouraging converts to share their stories of faith.

✤ *To develop within families and households the capacity to share the Gospel.*

Possible strategies:

- programs to support parents as the primary sharers of faith with their children;
- family outreach to other families to experience the Good News of Jesus;
- training programs so that families, individually or in support groups, can learn more effective methods of sharing the Gospel; and
- fostering regular family prayer and share time.

- *To equip and empower our active Catholic members to exercise their baptismal call to evangelize.*

  Possible strategies:
  - renewal days;
  - witness training;
  - training of Catholics for one-to-one evangelization;
  - use of baptismal and sacramental preparation to expand understandings of discipleship;
  - modeling and witness from those involved in the Rite of Christian Initiation of Adults;
  - evangelization components in religious education materials;
  - parish missions; and
  - preparing specially designated people as full-time evangelizers.

- *To use special times in parish and family life to invite people to faith.*

  Possible strategies:
  - inviting young families to share about forming their young children in faith;
  - special ministry to young adults in parishes and college campuses;
  - emphasizing the evangelizing dimension of youth ministry for middle school and high school students; and
  - involving youth and families in ministries of faith and service to others.

- *To cultivate an active core of the baptized to serve as ministers of evangelization in their parishes, dioceses, neighborhoods, workplaces, and homes.*

  Possible strategies:
  - formation of diocesan evangelization committees and offices;
  - formation of evangelization teams in parishes;
  - formation and support of national and regional schools of evangelization; and
  - workshops and support groups for those involved in evangelization in a more explicit way.

- *To invite effectively people to our Church.*

  Possible strategies on the national level:
  - careful input into the images that are projected about the Church through the media;
  - the recruitment of Catholics skilled in media to assist in this new imaging;
  - care for the evangelizing dimension of every official church pronouncement; and
  - the development of national media campaigns describing the Catholic Church.

  On a more local level:
  - mailings, home visits, consistent invitation to people newly moving into parish areas;

- neighborhood publicity through newspapers and posters;
- periodic taking of a census;
- involvement in and service to the neighborhood;
- development of neighborhood, parish, and local events to which people would be specially invited, be they open houses, open forums for airing questions and issues, events for friends or extended families, or other programs of welcoming; and
- greater sensitivity to the needs of the seeker.

✣ *To design programs of outreach for those who have ceased being active in the Church.*

Possible strategies:

- development of programs to help people experience reconciliation;
- renewed celebration of the sacrament of reconciliation;
- programs for the divorced, separated, and those who feel alienated from the Church;
- professional surveys of inactive Catholics;
- development of ministries that emphasize the mercy and compassion of God; and
- parish missions.

✣ *To design programs that reach out in particular ways to those who do not participate in a church community or who seek the fullness of faith.*

Possible strategies:

- formation of new, innovative methods of inquiry in the period before the catechumenate;
- special programs of hospitality and welcome, whether at the local church or in homes;
- exploration of new forms of Catholic presence in cities, suburban malls, storefronts, and other places of congregation;
- personal visits; and
- regional mailings.

✣ *To foster cultural diversity within the unity of the Church.*

Possible strategies:

- serious review of diocesan policies about parish organization, leadership, and empowerment to ensure that newcomers to our land have a place in the Church;
- training of clergy and ministers in needed foreign languages;
- programs to advance greater understanding of cultural diversity;
- while ensuring the unity of the Church, efforts to help newcomers to our land to develop their own social and church structures; and
- joint celebrations of the many cultures represented in our parishes, especially on great feast days, to reflect the Catholic scope of our lives.

✣ *To deepen ecumenical involvement.*

Possible strategies:

- careful collaboration with local and state ecumenical agencies;
- joint study of Roman Catholic and other Christian dialogues touching on evangelization, mission, and proselytism;
- study of Roman Catholic understandings of and approaches to Judaism;
- developing sensitivities to interreligious relationship and Roman Catholic teaching on dialogue and proclamation;
- mutual dialogue and sharing;
- joint scriptural study and social justice projects;
- shared discussion groups and socials; and
- where appropriate, joint services of prayer and devotion.

Goal III: To foster gospel values in our society, promoting the dignity of the human person, the importance of the family, and the common good of our society so that our nation may continue to be transformed by the saving power of Jesus Christ.

This goal follows upon the other two: the appreciation of our faith and its spread should lead to the transformation of our society. The pursuit of this goal, however, must accompany the pursuit of the other two because evangelization is not possible without powerful signs of justice and peace, as the Gospel shapes the framework of our lives. The Catholic Church has developed a strong social doctrine concerning the common good—a tradition based on the proper ordering of society and supporting the inalienable dignity of every person. In the United States, this tradition has been cultivated in the advocacy of religious liberty; the pursuit of social justice, especially for those left out of today's society; just economic policies; a consistent ethic of human life; and striving for peace in a nuclear world.

This goal means supporting those cultural elements in our land that reflect Catholic values and challenging those that reject it. Catholics, who today are involved in every level of modern life in the United States, have to address our society as a system and also in particular situations.

The transformation of our society in Christ particularly calls for the involvement and skills of lay men and women who carry the values of the Gospel into their homes, workplaces, areas of recreation—indeed, into all aspects of life.[57]

This goal requires the strategy of strengthening our everyday involvement with those in need, of reflecting on the workplace and media, and of encouraging Catholic involvement in areas of public policy as a way of having greater impact on society's values.

Goal III entails the following objectives:

❖ *To involve parishes and local service groups in the needs of their neighborhood.*

Possible strategies:

- raising the awareness of Catholics of the needs of the poor and marginal;
- making works of justice and love priorities in our parishes and other agencies;
- organizing the service of almost every Catholic in these works;
- engagement in ecumenical agencies committed to the common good;
- expansion of works of charity and help for the needy; and
- setting specific targets for parish or diocesan involvement in works of service to meet immediate human needs.

❖ *To foster the importance of the family.*

Possible strategies:

- marriage preparation and support for young married couples;
- family retreats and other religious experiences;
- spiritual, personal, social, and financial counseling for families;
- couple-to-couple faith sharing;
- support groups and networking for families; and
- influencing social policy to strengthen family life.

❖ *To develop groups to explore issues of the workplace and lay spirituality.*

Possible strategies:

- workshops on evangelization in the workplace;
- support groups for professionals;
- retreats on the value of work and the ethical/justice issues associated with employment; and
- renewal days organized by and for lay people.

❖ *To encourage Catholic witness in the arts and in the American intellectual community.*

Possible strategies:

- development of the arts as a way to proclaim the Gospel;
- formation of faith support groups for artists;
- promotion of gospel values in Catholic institutions of higher learning; and
- support of campus ministries in their Christian witness to institutions of higher learning.

✣ *To involve every Catholic, on different levels, in areas of public policy.*

Possible strategies:

- parish education programs with a social justice component;
- study and education about political choices that Catholics make;
- voter registration drives;
- support groups for professional Catholics and other Christians, particularly in areas of law, economics, and social services; and
- encouraging lay people to run for and hold public office.

✣ *To involve the Catholic Church, on every level, in the media.*

Possible strategies:

- development of media plans for evangelization on the national, local, and parochial levels;
- use of audio, video, and videotapes to communicate the Catholic faith to others;
- reflection on Catholics' *use* of the media in their homes, workplaces, and educational settings;
- formation of task forces of Catholics and other Christians involved in communications in various regions to discuss questions of values in the media and the impact Christian people can have on them;
- the involvement of bishops and other religious leaders as public spokespersons of the Church through local print and broadcast media; and
- cultivation of cable television, optical storage, computer and other technology for communicating the Gospel and Christian values.

✣ *To involve Catholics, at every level, in questions of economic systems.*

Possible strategies:

- use of professional resources in the parish and diocese to raise questions about economic systems and their consequences concerning the dominant issues of justice, particularly homelessness, social inequities, educational opportunities, housing and employment, and racial equality; and
- forming ministries to deal with unjust economic systems and practices.

An Invitation

One of the earliest stories of Jesus finds him walking along the shore; he sees two people, and then two others, all of them working as fishermen. "Come after me," he says. And, once they followed the Christ, their lives became part of the story of salvation.[58]

We offer the Catholics of the United States the same invitation as Jesus: Come and follow! Come, hear the Lord calling each one of us; come, follow the Teacher who makes us his disciples. Come, be part of the story of salvation.

Our invitation asks every believer to discover ways that he or she can realize this plan in every way appropriate—personally, in the family, in the neighborhood and parish, or as part of a larger organization.

Make the goals of this plan real. Discover how the Spirit is leading you to evangelize. Search out how it can reshape our parishes and our institutions. To do this takes questioning and searching, discovery and decision. But, most of all, it takes faith. Pray that God's Holy Spirit will give Catholics in this nation the kind of faith needed to begin evangelizing seriously.

We invite you: Make this plan *your* plan.

Structures for Implementation

Because this plan must involve every one of us, we bishops first of all pledge to implement it ourselves. We pledge, as shepherds of God's people, to proclaim the Good News of Jesus Christ through welcome, mercy, and renewal. We pledge to continue being evangelized by the Gospel of Jesus as we meet him in our people and in the challenges of today's world.

We commit ourselves to adding new full-time staff for evangelization at the National Conference of Catholic Bishops in Washington, D.C. to help dioceses and other church agencies carry out the goals of this plan and strategy. As pastors of local churches, we realize that individuals and parishes also need support at the diocesan level. Each bishop will seriously consider establishing a diocesan office and an evangelization committee or otherwise assign staff to give the ministry of evangelization proper visibility and attention, as well as provide resources for evangelization to his people. Parishes will be looking to these offices for direction and materials.

We will work together with our brother priests and parish leaders to formulate plans and strategies in the local churches which will carry forward our common ministry of evangelization.

Discover how the Spirit is leading you to evangelize. . . . Pray that God's Holy Spirit will give Catholics in this nation the kind of faith needed to begin evangelizing seriously.

Bishops should take every occasion to speak out on the need and duty of every Catholic to be an evangelizer. Because we need everyone's help to implement this plan, we ask our brother and sister Catholics to support us in the following ways:

1. Each individual Catholic is to look at his or her everyday life from the viewpoint of evangelization. Take note of the many opportunities to support another's faith, to share faith, and to help build up Jesus' kingdom in our homes and workplaces, among our neighbors and friends. Catholics should participate in renewal programs and receive training in evangelization.

2. Families must find ways to highlight the faith that is part of their daily life, until each family unit knows itself as a "domestic church" living and sharing faith. If each household lived a vibrant faith, the members would more naturally reach out to their friends and neighbors, introducing them by their lives to the faith of Christ Jesus. Households are invited to see the dynamics of welcoming, sharing, caring, and nourishing as dynamics of evangelization. Families, individually or together, should read this plan with a view to helping them both appreciate and revitalize the practice of faith in the family and in the neighborhood.

3. Parishes, as part of their regular planning process, need to examine their activities in light of this plan. They should consider how to give their present ministry a clearer evangelizing focus and how new ministries might be formed to achieve the goals of this plan. Each parish should have an evangelization team trained and prepared to help the whole parish implement the goals and objectives of this plan. These teams could help train Catholics in evangelization and provide resources to individuals, families, and parish groups. Parishes might even consider designating a trained person as a full-time coordinator of evangelization.

We ask parish leadership, especially pastors who have a critical leadership role, to understand their ministry in terms of this plan. We commit ourselves to support pastors in the implementation of this plan by special gatherings to hear their concerns, assess their needs, and address their issues. We recognize how burdened parish leadership is today; our hope is that this plan can actually clarify the purpose of parish leadership and thereby ease the burdens of already busy pastors.

4. Catholic institutions are also to review their goals in light of this plan. They should review the ways they can, through the services they provide, reflect the Good News of Jesus. Schools and hospitals, often the only face of the Church some people see, need to look at how their staffs welcome and treat people. Ways in which people can be invited to know Jesus and the Church through these institutions should be constantly explored and reviewed. From our manner of welcoming, enlisting, and serving people, all Catholic institutions should be signs of the kingdom of Christ. Catholics enjoy a tremendous reputation in serving the most basic human needs; along with that, should we not also enjoy a reputation for sharing our Catholic faith?

5. Local, diocesan, and national organizations need to renew their own mission with a view to evangelization. Millions of Catholics belong to Catholic organizations; their membership can lead them to a greater pursuit of Catholic goals. Cannot the goals of our plan find an echo in the goals of your organization? Your support, both nationally and locally, will be a tremendous asset to the Church.

A Concluding Prayer

As we present this plan to our brother and sister Catholics in the United States, we pray that, through the Holy Spirit, it may be a means of bringing renewal to our Church and new life to all who search for God. We have felt the hunger of our nation for God and the Gospel of Jesus as we have developed this plan and strategy. As this plan is read, studied, and implemented, may it help all Catholics know the hunger for faith in today's society.

We pray that our Catholic people will be set ablaze with a desire to live their faith fully and share it freely with others. May their eagerness to share the faith bring a transformation to our nation and, with missionary dedication, even to the whole world. We ask God to open the heart of every Catholic, to see the need for the Gospel in each life, in our nation and on our planet.

We ask Mary, the one through whom Jesus entered our world, to guide us in presenting Jesus to those who live in our land. May her prayers help us to share in her courage and faithfulness. May they lead us to imitate her discipleship, her turning to Jesus, her love for God and for all. May the compassion that Mary has always reflected be present in our hearts.

We also pray that, like the disciples walking that Easter morning to Emmaus, all Catholics may feel their hearts burning through the presence of Jesus.[59] As those two disciples felt the presence of Jesus in their journey, we ask that the ministry of evangelizing help believers feel anew the presence of Jesus and help others discover his gracious presence.

We pray that the fire of Jesus enkindled in us by God's Spirit may lead more and more people in our land to become disciples, formed in the image of Christ our Savior.

Resources

Church Documents on Evangelization

Encounters with Faith: A Handbook for the Observance of the Fifth Centenary of Evangelization in the Americas (Washington, D.C.: United States Catholic Conference, 1991).

Here I Am, Send Me: A Conference Response to the Evangelization of African Americans and the "National Black Catholic Pastoral Plan" (Washington, D.C.: United States Catholic Conference, 1987).

Heritage and Hope: Evangelization in the United States (Washington, D.C.: United States Catholic Conference, 1991).

National Pastoral Plan for Hispanic Ministry (Washington, D.C.: United States Catholic Conference, 1987).

On Evangelization in the Modern World, Apostolic Exhortation of Paul VI (Washington, D.C.: United States Catholic Conference, 1975).

On the Permanent Validity of the Church's Missionary Mandate, Encyclical Letter of John Paul II (Washington, D.C.: United States Catholic Conference, 1991).

To the Ends of the Earth: A Pastoral Statement on World Mission, Statement of the U.S. Bishops (Washington, D.C.: United States Catholic Conference, 1986).

Other Church Documents

Catechism of the Catholic Church (Washington, D.C.: United States Catholic Conference, 1993).

"Dialogue and Proclamation: Reflections and Orientations on Interreligious Dialogue and the Proclamation of the Gospel of Jesus Christ," *Origins* 21:8 (July 4, 1991).

Economic Justice for All: Pastoral Letter on Catholic Social Teaching and the U.S. Economy (Washington, D.C.: United States Catholic Conference, 1986).

A Family Perspective in Church and Society: A Manual for All Pastoral Leaders (Washington, D.C.: United States Catholic Conference, 1988).

Families at the Center: A Handbook for Parish Ministry with a Family Perspective (Washington, D.C.: United States Catholic Conference, 1988).

God's Mercy Endures Forever: Guidelines on the Presentation of Jews and Judaism in Catholic Preaching (Washington, D.C.: United States Catholic Conference, 1988).

Notes on the Correct Way to Present the Jews and Judaism in Preaching and Catechesis of the Roman Catholic Church [Commission on Religious Relations with the Jews] (Washington, D.C.: United States Catholic Conference, 1985).

On the Family, Apostolic Exhortation of John Paul II (Washington, D.C.: United States Catholic Conference, 1981).

On the Vocation and the Mission of the Lay Faithful in the Church and in the World, Post-Synodal Apostolic Exhortation of John Paul II (Washington, D.C.: United States Catholic Conference, 1989).

Pastoral Statement of U.S. Catholic Bishops on Persons with Disabilities (Washington, D.C.: United States Catholic Conference, 1978).

The Rite of Christian Initiation of Adults (Washington, D.C.: United States Catholic Conference, 1988).

To order these resources or to obtain a catalog of other USCC titles, call toll-free 1-800-235-8722. In the Washington metropolitan area or from outside the United States, call 301-209-9020.

Notes

1. Mark 10:46-52.
2. Luke 7:2-9.
3. John 4:7-42.
4. Luke 10:38-45; John 11:1-45.
5. *On Evangelization in the Modern World* (*Evangelii Nuntiandi*), 14.
6. Ibid., 18.
7. Ibid., 22.
8. Matthew 5:13.
9. Romans 5:12-21.
10. *On the Permanent Validity of the Church's Missionary Mandate* (*Redemptoris Missio*), 33.
11. *On Evangelization in the Modern World,* 24.
12. Matthew 28:20.
13. Matthew 25:40.
14. Acts 9:5.
15. Matthew 28:18-20.
16. John 1:1; 1:14.
17. Hebrews 1:3.
18. 1 Corinthians 1:24.
19. Philippians 2:7.
20. Philippians 2:8-9.
21. John 14:6.
22. John 14:10.
23. Luke 10:21.
24. John 17:21.
25. *On the Permanent Validity of the Church's Missionary Mandate*, 9.
26. Ibid.
27. Luke 5:6.
28. Luke 6:38.
29. Matthew 23:37.
30. Acts 1:8.
31. John 20:22.
32. *On Evangelization in the Modern World,* 75.
33. Zephaniah 3:9; Isaiah 66:23; Psalm 65:4; Romans 11:11-32.
34. *On Evangelization in the Modern World,* 19.
35. *On the Hundredth Anniversary of "Rerum Novarum"* (*Centesimus Annus*), 5.
36. *Dogmatic Constitution on the Church* (*Lumen Gentium*), 1.
37. *On the Vocation and Mission of the Lay Faithful in the Church and in the World* (*Christifideles Laici*), 17 and 34.
38. *On the Permanent Validity of the Church's Missionary Mandate,* 3.
39. *National Pastoral Plan for Hispanic Ministry* (Washington, D.C.: United States Catholic Conference, 1988).
40. *Here I Am, Send Me: A Conference Response to the Evangelization of African Americans and the "National Black Catholic Pastoral Plan"* (Washington, D.C.: United States Catholic Conference, 1988).
41. *Heritage and Hope: Evangelization in the United States* (Washington, D.C.: United States Catholic Conference, 1991).
42. See Matthew 3:13-17 and John 1:29-34.
43. Mark 1:12.
44. Cf. Romans 6:3-4.
45. Acts 2:1-4.
46. Luke 1:26-38.
47. Matthew 16:13-16.
48. Mark 14:66-72.
49. Acts 2:14ff.
50. John 21:18-19.
51. Acts 2:1-14.
52. Matthew 7:11.
53. Matthew 7:7-8.
54. *On Evangelization in the Modern World,* 60.
55. *Dogmatic Constitution on the Church,* 40.
56. 1 Corinthians 15:28.
57. *On Evangelization in the Modern World,* 70-73; and *On the Vocation and Mission of the Lay Faithful in the Church and in the World,* 15.
58. Mark 1:14-20.
59. Luke 24:13-35.